A Coventry Tale:
The Golden Thread

Paul A M Palmer

Copyright © 2023 Paul A M Palmer
All rights reserved.
ISBN-13: 9798455337772

Cover Photograph Copyright © 2020 Paul A M Palmer
All rights reserved.

Cover Image Copyright © 2023 Steve Milner
All rights reserved.

Illustrations Copyright © 2023 Steve Milner
All rights reserved.

This book is dedicated to the City and people of Coventry, past and present.

CONTENTS

Introduction 1
Historical Notes & List of Characters 2
Narrator's Prologue 5
A Falcon's Eye View 7
Lain Like A Stone 9
Good Morning Bela! 11
Narrator (Sinners or Saints?) 13
Conspiracy 15
Aries 17
Gold (Part 1) 19
Dark Wood 21
Taurus 23
A Tale To Tell (Part 1) 25
A Tale To Tell (Part 2) 27
Exposed 29
Gemini 31
Gold (Part 2) 33
Recipe for Love 35
Cancer 37
Pin 39
Sweet Love 41
Catching Teardrops 43
Leo 45

Candle	47
Can it be True?	49
All Anew	51
Gigges A-Whirl	53
Virgo	55
A Tale to Tell (Part 3)	57
A Tale to Tell (Part 4)	59
Lover's Lips	61
Libra	63
Running an Errand	65
Narrator (Hiding in the Eaves)	67
Gold (Part 3)	69
Gold (Part 4)	71
Scorpio	73
Jabet's Ash (Part 1)	75
When Fortune Smiles	77
Jabet's Ash (Part 2)	79
Jabet's Ash (Part 3)	81
Sagittarius	83
Narrator (Counting Blessings)	85
Among The Stars	87
Farewell	89
Gold (Part 5)	91
Narrator (The Air is Clear)	93
Capricorn	95

Bury All Deep 97
Aquarius 99
Limbrick Wood (Part 1) 101
Pisces 103
Limbrick Wood (Part 2) 105
Riddle I Can Solve 107
Narrator (Story's Ending) 109
Felicity of My Heart 111

ACKNOWLEDGEMENTS

As ever, love and thanks go to Fliss as Editor-in-Chief and for listening to the many revisions of each work. I'm equally indebted to my good friend Steve for insights, edits and brilliant illustrations to help bring the poetry to life.

Special thanks also go to staff at the Reference Library in the Herbert Art Gallery in Coventry for helping with the foundations for this series of books.

Finally, much love and thanks go to my family and friends for their constant support and encouragement.

Introduction

This sequel to *'A Coventry Tale ... woven in poetry'* is, again, a work of fiction. As in the previous book, the characters continue to interact with each other, but with a different storyline or two.

I have tried to ensure that the language is consistent with the 15th century, but mixed with a contemporary style and sticking with (for example) *mayhap* instead of *perhaps* for a more authentic approach for each character.

The style of the poetry is intentionally contemporary in nature, so poems *spoken* by the characters and ballads *performed* by the minstrel in this book do not conform to those of the period. Unlike the previous book, all poems within are newly written.

There are a couple of plots running through the book, but the intention is to keep the overall narrative flowing, so the characters simply interact as and when.

I am pleased once more to have such wonderful illustrations sitting alongside the words in this book, helping to bring them to life, thanks to the admirable talents of the artist.

I hope you enjoy reading this sequel to and feel inspired to visit Coventry or to follow one of the references listed in the *Author's Notes* section at the end of the book.

Historical Notes & List of Characters

The Leet Court

Coventry was ruled by its *Leet Court* from circa 1425 until the dissolution of the monasteries (1536-1541). The *Leet Court* elected the Mayor and picked every trial jury, and organised the system of bailiffs. When the city wall was built, the *Court* collected the *murage* (wall tax) for its maintenance; details regarding taxes paid are in the *Leet Book,* translated and annotated by Mary Dormer Harris - see *References* for details.

The Gates

Coventry had twelve gates, spaced out along the length of the wall as it surrounded the city. New Gate was first, guarding the London Road approach. They are listed below:

- Bishop Gate
- Cook Street Gate
- Priory Gate
- Dern Gate (known as *Bastille Gate* in 1450)
- Gosford Gate
- New Gate
- Little Park Gate
- Cheylesmore Gate
- Greyfriars' Gate
- Spon Gate
- Hill Street Gate
- Well Street Gate

Mentioned in the poems:

a *gigge* is a spinning top;

an *owche* is a piece of lady's jewellery.

Shortly's Field may have been owned by John Shortly, the son of Dame Isabella Langley who lived in the Langley's house in Earl Street (circa 1473). According to the *Leet Book*, in 1424 Thomas Langley (Duke of Durham) was a member of the King's Council, so the family clearly had influence within the city.

List of Characters

The characters in *The Golden Thread* are mostly fictional with a couple of characters based on real people. Firstly, the fictional characters:

Addy: Guardsman, romantically involved with Maud.

Bela: Maud's niece, lives and works in *The Star* inn.

Clarice: Fabian's wife.

Dizzy: Simpleton who begs for a living, pitied by everyone.

Fabian: Wealthy heir on a secret mission for his father.

Jocelin: Resident minstrel (troubadour) at *The Star* inn.

Maud: Bela's Aunt and proud owner of *The Star* inn.

Odo: The Prior's summoner, despised by all.

The Conspirators: characters with zodiac code-names.

Tyrell: One of the conspirators.

The following characters are taken from the *Leet Book* and other sources (see *Author's Notes* section):

Richard Barbur - alchemist in St Nicholas Street, Coventry.

John Jabet - lived in Bishop Street ward in 1449.

Narrator's Prologue

Hello again, come follow me,
you're welcome back to Coventry!

Though time has ebbed and months gone by
'tis good to see we've caught your eye!

There's more to tell, yes, more to say,
so set aside your cares this day,

and like the best of tapestries,
the threads we weave mayhap will please.

A Falcon's Eye View

I see all those people,
from paupers to Prior -
    his steeples are high
    but I can climb higher.

I'm wary of tricks
to catch me in sacks,
    but most men are fools
    and cunning they lack.

So stay here a while,
and I'll be your guide -
    just follow my lead,
    through this story we'll glide.

We'll pick up this thread,
it's golden, they say,
    and cast off your cares
    for part of this day.

Some old names and new
have come to the fore,
    and we shall be looking
    beyond each locked door.

The plots they do thicken,
like a good mutton stew,
    so let us swoop down
    and see what's to do ...

Lain Like A Stone

Bela laments:

I have lain like a stone on the shore
counting the tides,

and still he has not come.

I have brooded like a boulder on
the steepest of hillsides,

and still he has not come.

I have waited with the trees while each
lost their lustre, suffering frost then snow
until every new leaf unfurls from bud,

and still he has not come.

I have watched the moon rise and fall, and
pleaded with the stars,

and still he has not come.

How long must I sit like a stone on the shore
watching the tides,

hoping that he will come?

Good Morning Bela!

Maud to Bela:

Oh, Bela, my sweetheart, 'tis time to be woken
you talk while asleep, for words I heard spoken!

Addy's awake now but just sat on his rump -
he's not good with mornings, the useless old lump!

Jocelin is humming - a ballad of love;
that lad never stops, thank heavens above!

Bela, my dear, please come out of your dream!
We have much to prepare and places to clean:

tankards to swill out and rushes to sweep -
'tis no time to lay there, my beauty, asleep!

The cobwebs need brushing now daylight is here;
that storm has passed over and the sky is now clear.

I see your sweet smile, you've awoken at last -
I'll fetch you some food and we shall break fast.

Our new ale is ready - old barrels need swilling -
your spirit looks groggy, but the flesh must be willing!

And I'll need you at market, we've provisions to glean,
with a pannier of Pippins, fit for a queen.

Narrator (Sinners or Saints?)

I can see from this tower,
    but 'tis dusk at this hour
    as men without horses arrive;

a gathering with whispers
    and pulling of whiskers
    as they huddle around and connive.

One seems to be leading,
    the others conceding,
    as the matter in hand is laid bare;

There are nods of consent
    as though all is well meant,
    yet one or two worriedly stare.

Bablake's the place -
    they've met here before
    and dusk is the time that they favour;

they take the same room
    few candles, much gloom,
    for the darkness is what they all savour.

I'm perched at St John's,
    though the night has now come
    'tis time that all here were sleeping;

now the candles are snuffed,
    these sinners or saints
    I'll watch steal away, all a-creeping.

Conspiracy

John Jabet:

In Bablake we've all gathered here
to swear our solemn vows,

all shadowed by St John's fine tower
while time and tide allows.

Each of you must seek your station,
with zodiac assigned,

and watchful eyes with listening ears
reporting all you find.

Now, while the dawn reveals itself
our secrets must stay hidden;

my home's amongst the elements
where I'll wait 'til I'm bidden.

A richer company soon we'll be,
purse bulging with gold delight,

though sober now, we wait and thirst,
but we'll drink come victory night!

Let candles' flames extinguished be
and oil lamps turned down low,

with whispered names and voices too,
'tis time, my friends, to go.

Aries

We each of us have different parts
as per the stars assigned,

and I must watch St Nicholas' Street,
look out for certain signs.

The alchemist takes no chances here
his home is locked up tight,

with locks and bolts and bars and more
to keep out all at night.

I am disguised in what I do,
a pedlar sharpening knives,

'tis easy rumbling up and down
and chatting to men's wives.

They tell me all about their men
how useless they all are,

they offer me warm beds as well,
but I haven't strayed that far!

For one eye on the alchemist
I must always keep,

waiting 'til his lights are out
before I take my sleep.

Gold (Part 1)

The Alchemist, Richard Barbur:

Welcome reader, welcome,
you will have to watch in awe,

and see me turn the basest parts
into gold without a flaw!

The elements I have to hand
and keep the charcoal burning -

the method's locked inside my mind,
after many years of learning.

The curtains keep it dark in here
in case the neighbours spy,

and though I'm jealous of my art
I wouldn't harm a fly!

Others they have tried and failed
'tis good that it is so,

for when success becomes my guest
my fame shall grow and grow!

Some sulphur, lead, a dash of salt
makes such a ghastly smell,

but in the end, I shall be rich
with so much gold to sell.

So, if you please I must away,
my patrons beckon me.

I'm sure that we shall meet again
when time and tide agree.

Dark Wood

Bela laments:

In a dark wood, wandering,
through this never-ending night,

my thoughts are dark as storm-clouds
as I struggle with my plight.

I crush beneath my feet
many dreams I once held dear -

the leaves of fallen wishes,
of hope no longer here.

I search for precious moments
of perfect clarity -

I've lost my way and stumbled,
now I yearn for charity.

Maud may now disown me
when she knows of my shame,

Addy too will rage a while
and wish to pin the blame.

So, I'm in this dark wood, wondering
if I'll ever see the light,

and I pray for some salvation
from an ever-darkening night.

Taurus

I'm the eyes and ears at the fat Prior's table,
slipping away just as soon as I'm able,

picking up scraps that might just matter
from all those engaged in loose, idle chatter.

Dawdling near stairways, or hiding in shadows
watching these folks take the strangest bedfellows.

But where are the friends of this most irksome man -
who could they be and what is their plan?

We have our own, my brothers and me,
all carefully worked out as you will soon see.

At least there's a fire and there's plenty of meat,
the odd cup of wine when I get time to eat;

the others will struggle to have such delights,
so I count my blessings each day and each night!

I peek through the threadbare - in cloaks they arrive
to dine with the Prior, hoping one day they'll thrive.

Ah, here are some rich folk and now I must mingle,
mayhap I'll find truths to make our plot tingle.

A Tale To Tell (Part 1)

Maud to Bela:

Bela, come, tell me please all that is wrong -
we'll go upstairs, and leave this loud throng.

Pray, speak of the troubles in your saddened heart,
and you must be truthful; please sit here and start.

I fear I may know of your tale but do wish
to hear it, my dearest, from your own sweet lips.

And now I can see those bleak tears they do call,
I know 'tis the time for all veils to fall.

For I too was a maiden, distressed, just like you,
and deeply in love with a young lad so true,

but a war came between us and broke that sweet bond,
though in my poor heart I stayed ever-fond.

To Lincoln I journeyed, 'twas fearful and slow,
to have my own babe that I have ever loved so.

Oh, I cherished my daughter from that day back then,
and watched her far closer than a good mother hen!

And so here you are, my own beautiful girl -
I see that your thoughts must be all a-whirl.

But you must dry your eyes and please do not fret,
for this story of yours has no ending yet.

A Tale To Tell (Part 2)

Bela to Maud:

These tears are happily spiced with joy, for you have
indeed been mother and more to me all these years,

and now I have brought you this shame.
Forgive me, Maud, *Mother*, I mean.

It seems an age since our lips met, Fabian's hand
in mine upon a secret bedding; and how time has
slowed, as people come and go.

I still have my keepsakes and memory of his
many promises to return, but he has not.

Yet every day I miss him more and more,
like a seedling for the rain that's falling now.

And how I envy that seedling, as I wait by
the window, watching the drops disturb the
puddles, ignorant of the trouble I'm in.

'Tis not the only thing growing slowly and silently
and soon to show itself to all the world.

But when these tears are dried, you and I shall still be
daughter and mother, bearing and sharing secrets,

and taking comfort in this new-found bond between
us, and I shall no longer be *The Orphan of The Star*.

Exposed

The Falcon shares his thoughts:
I kept your secrets,
    whispered in shadows
    under a waxing moon's watchful glare.

Others may have heard -
    a fox has ears, a hunting owl
    watching its prey closely.

I told no-one your truths,
    carrying them like gems
    to a jeweller, close to my heart.

Others may have noticed:
    glancing servants; a mother knows
    her daughter's mood.

I beheld your fears,
    fragile as a chick before its prey,
    but I did not pounce.

Others have exposed you:
    by luck have heard or seen or
    guessed, but on my life
and those of my chicks,
    it was not me. I kept your secrets;
    I told no-one.

Gemini

The hermitage is bleak and grim
and no-one travels there within -

I'm stuck out here on Gosford Green
trying hard to stay unseen.

'Tis cramp I suffer from the most
with eyes upon this damn'd outpost.

We all drew lots and this is mine -
some others spy in places fine,

with wenches serving treats and more,
a nice warm bed and fire that roars,

while I must mingle with the mud
and listen for those hooves that thud,

and then I shall recount my tale
refreshed and warmed by finest ale.

Sometimes the birds do chirp or sing
while I do ponder golden things,

forget these scratching thorns and briars
and dream that ladies call me 'Sire'.

Thank God! A horse! I soon may flee,
and make my way to Coventry.

Gold (Part 2)

Richard Barbur:

Dear reader, pray, you should be still
while bellows I must work.

My patrons, they are pleased with me
(though one or two seem irked).

It takes great skill and learning thus,
to make such things transform,

folks will nod as if they know,
but they are like a swarm

of bees that buzz in aimless flight
not knowing where to land,

so I must guide them carefully
and take them all in hand.

I answer truthful as I can
but secrets I withhold -

there are no shortcuts I can take
as they have oft been told!

The flames must keep the charcoal hot
or all my work's in vain,

'tis all part of the mystery -
and that I tell you plain!

Dear Jove, but this is tiring work,
I think you must move on.

And I shall have a well-earned rest
when certain you have gone!

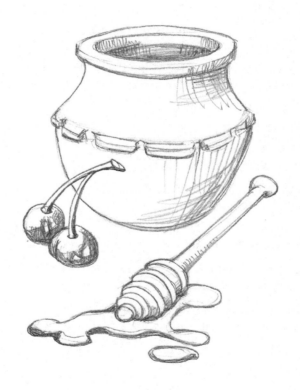

Recipe for Love

Jocelin sings (ad nauseum) to the drinkers at The Star:

Call me to your kitchen, lady, any time you can;
pull me to your pantry, lady,
let me be your man!

Show me all your secret spices -
I shall help you mix,
then we'll blend them all together -
share each other's tricks!

Call me to your kitchen, lady, any time you can;
pull me to your pantry, lady,
let me be your man!

Let us weigh the flour and butter -
throw surprises in,
see how we can pass the time
like dough that keeps a-rising!

Call me to your kitchen, lady, any time you can;
pull me to your pantry, lady,
let me be your man!

When the baking time is up
and our hunger is no more,
let us savour what we've made
upon that pantry floor.

So, call me to your kitchen, lady, any time you can;
pull me to your pantry, lady,
let me be your man!

Cancer

From Shortly's Field to Langley's house,
I travelled late last night;

I play the part of motley fool
and look a pretty sight.

There's none that would suspect my truth,
that I'm in search so bold

for those who pay the alchemist
to make them rich with gold.

I tumble here and fumble there,
a smile and giggle make,

and all the while those gathered round
know not that I'm a snake;

for I shall bite with venom strong
when time and tide allow,

and others see my worth at last -
that promise I avow.

I offer jests, for I have wit -
enough and more to spare;

the ladies with their lords in tow
do laugh without a care.

Some kindly offer me a wink,
and others toss a coin,

but I must simply bide my time,
'til gold I can purloin.

Pin

Bela laments:

When truth's laid bare, what will folks say
when I do serve them every day?

Wagging tongues and pointing fingers,
ever-after stares that linger.

Whispers, words of hateful spite
from dawn 'til dusk and then each night.

What will Maud and Addy think?
Mayhap they both shall take to drink.

And when I sleep, my dreams are grim
I wake and hope for word from him,

but none has come, that candle's burned -
my heart at last from him has turned.

I'll creep down to our silent yard
and ponder on my troubles hard.

'Tis early morn, the Inn is still -
I hear the sound of distant mills;

I see a pin and pick it up
and hope this day shall bring me luck.

Here's Jocelin who's smiled my way
and looks like he has words to say.

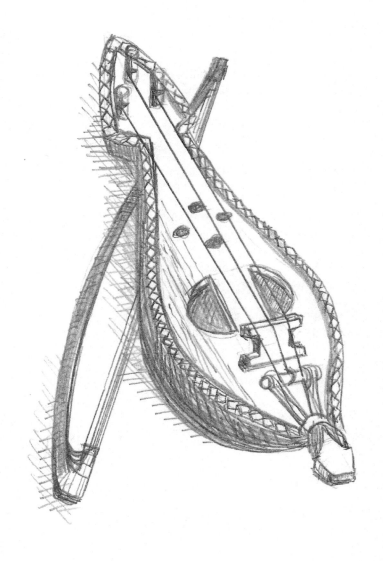

Sweet Love

Jocelin to Bela:

New words I've written
with melody too

I shall sing them most softly
then ask: what think you?

Sweet love, my beloved,
bringing spring to my winters;

sweet love, my beloved,
bringing honey to my splinters;

sweet love, my beloved,
bringing colour to my meadows;

sweet love, my beloved,
bringing light to my shadows;

sweet love, my beloved,
bringing song to my days;

bringing love, my beloved,
in so many ways.

Catching Teardrops

Bela to Jocelin:

Jocelin your words are sweet,
they bring me tears of joy;

such truths are spoken rare in love
betwixt a girl and boy.

Your melody is honeyed dew
like ale, refreshing clear;

a melancholy heart have I
but you have warmed me dear.

I always listen carefully -
your songs do stir the heart,

for here you catch my teardrops thus
and have done since the start.

I fear that you will turn away
when all my faults are known,

and foulest words are spoken true
then me you may disown.

Leo

Lingering by The Drapery, the merchants I can see;

I know of each and every one,
but they will not know me.

Among the finest cloths for sale a benefactor hides;

I play a game of patience, thus,
and time here I must bide.

The buyers are of merchant stock beyond the usual number -

'tis hard to count them one by one
without recourse to slumber!

I see the pilgrims come and go, mayhap they are disguised,

but I have also played that part -
they cannot fool the wise!

And when the gold is in my grasp, my wisdom I shall use

and choose my friends most carefully
for fear of what I'd lose.

Oh, time and tide, my share I'll spend on cloths of finest red,

But wait, I see that shifty Sire,
whose messenger has fled ...

Candle

Jocelin to Bela:

As every precious candle should have its special flame
I burn to hear your gentle voice
come calling out my name.

Your joy is summer's sunshine, despite the darkest day,
your laughter calms each tempest
whene'er they blow my way.

As freshly picked out flowers do light the dullest rooms,
to look upon your kindly face
dispels my deepest gloom.

Your smiles are like fine jewels, that sparkle so and shine,
and I would give you all I have
if only you'd be mine.

Your eyes do offer promises I hope that you would keep,
and arms that bring me bliss-filled dreams
where I wish that I could sleep.

With footsteps oh-so-graceful I would have you at my side,
the child you bear I'd call my own
and marry you with pride.

Can it be True?

Bela to Jocelin:

I must be dreaming still, I fear,
or has the sky stopped falling here?

Are you beyond your wits, God-send,
to share my burden to the end?

Shall all my troubles wash away
like muddied streets on rainy days?

Oh Jocelin, might such joy come
as storm clouds part and bring the sun?

For now my mind is lost in thoughts,
enslaved they were, 'ere freedom bought

by your kind deed as offered here,
though I must ponder and be clear.

Tomorrow night at curfew's bell
I shall to you my answer tell.

All Anew

Bela to Jocelin:

Since yesterday's sweet song of love,
I've thought and prayed to God above.

My heart beats faster, yes, it's true,
knowing, soon, I'll be with you.

The fear has gone, I'm all anew -
I want to spend my days with you.

Sealed with a kiss that God may bless,
My answer true this day is "Yes!"

We must tell Maud, for she may guess,
and if she asks, I would confess.

Our secret then, until that day,
now back to work - I must away,

for you have songs to sing and play
and I shall plan our wedding day!

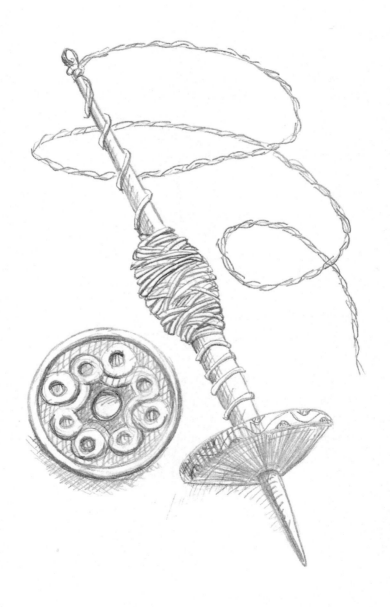

Gigges A-Whirl

Jocelin to Bela:

Bela, I am yours, forever true,
let kisses meet and gigges a-whirl,
my sweet and lovely, precious girl.

Let laughter sound;
let smiles be found -

here's mine for you,
unwrapped and true.

Forever yours as you are mine,
our kisses meet as gigges a-whirl,
my sweet and lovely, precious girl.

As loud as thunder
let church-bells ring;

let love be in the
songs we sing,

and be it known by all that

I am forever yours as you are mine,
so let kisses meet and gigges a-whirl,
my sweet and lovely, precious girl.

Virgo

Spicer Stoke's the place for me,
nearby Holy Trinity -
a greedy goldsmith's bound to wish
for a bit of alchemy!

'Tis busy in this little street
with gentle folk all spending,
dressed up in such finery,
their wealth seems never-ending.

My brothers in this venture great,
are bound by secrets grim;
our leader is a warrior, so
we dare not trouble him.

He came to us with plots and plans
for "Gold to make us rich."
We left our meeting place so quiet,
the night as black as pitch.

Our names are unimportant here -
we watch the City streets,
with star signs guiding all we do
to witness all who meet,

and making notes of all they say
and where they go to next,
for if we fail in this, our task,
our Captain will be vexed!

And there goes Goldsmith Number Four
a busy man this day!
So, I must follow for a while
but will he work or play?

A Tale to Tell (Part 3)

Maud to Addy:

Addy, I must whisper, keeping soft and low
words I should have uttered oh so long ago.

When you and I were young and our love was so new
my life was always full of joy when it was spent with you.

But deadly war did drag you so from our honeyed bed -
and I was left alone and lost, and then with child, unwed.

To save us both from shame and Odo's endless scorn
I headed to another town and there I wept and mourned.

But then a babe I had, thank God, and such a beauty too,
I've loved her every day since then and even more for you.

I see you know what I must say, or mayhap you might guess,
and so we thank the Lord above for love that He has blessed:

for Bela she is not my niece, she is our daughter true,
her joy to me is purest gold and now I'm telling you.

For now, she knows no truth I've told except a mother's part,
'tis time for me to say much more to warm her kindly heart.

But you, my love, until I do, be sure through thick and thin,
to alter not your countenance, but lose that lovesick grin!

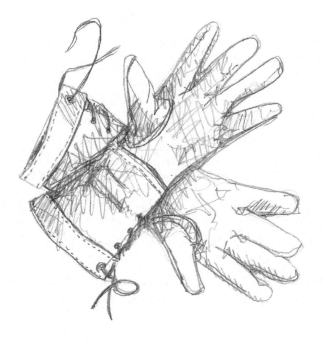

A Tale to Tell (Part 4)

Maud to Bela:

You must sit down beside me -
stop fretting around;

come, take my hand,
share the joy, be unbound.

You may not have guessed
what I'm here for to-day:

but Addy's your father
though he's too shy to say!

He is a proud one, that's certain,
you can tell from his grin!

Should you need his advice
just remember he's kin!

He does not know your secret,
for it's not mine to tell,

but the time will soon come
when he'll notice the swell.

Trust my judgement, dear Bela,
this isn't a curse,

and we'll all stick together,
so, fear not the worst.

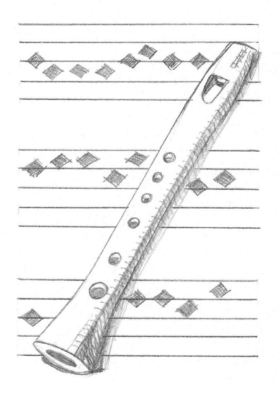

Lover's Lips

Jocelin sings:

With a lover's lips she led me on
to places far from here,

with endless kisses soft and sweet
each hour seem'd like a year.

To countries strange and fair we flew,
embraced, entwined in dreams,

where she, adorned in finest clothes;
her eyes, like jewels, gleamed.

And I, the richer man with her
brought gifts of purest gold.

We lived there in that happy state -
our love was true and bold.

How long, how long, the candles burned
I truly do not know,

caresses, care-free on that bed
like seas that ebbed and flowed.

Too soon, too soon, the time had fled -
our lover's lips must part,

But soon, but soon, again my love,
we shall meet heart to heart.

Libra

Corpus Christi's guildsmen have not yet noticed me,

beside St Nicholas' hall,
I loiter filled with glee.

These rich and powerful men with coin and more to spend

will mayhap send a messenger
which I shall apprehend.

Our alchemist has secret friends - we must discover who,

and follow them with muffled step
to see what they might do.

Our mystery man (we know not who) - to find him is a must,

and every scrap that we can glean
adds to our Captain's trust.

How shall I spend my fortune? Ah, that you may well ask -

I have not given too much thought
behind this well-worn mask!

Methinks I'll go to Ireland, for I have family there,

and with such gold as there will be
I'll have much land to spare,

and all who know me as their kin shall be set up with farms.

But until then outside this hall,
disguised, I'm selling charms!

Running an Errand

Fabian (to himself):

I'm back here at last, coming in from the cold -

I'm still running errands,
forced to do as I'm told.

I brought my wife, Clarice, along for this trip -

my mother insisted
with her usual grit.

I hope to see Bela, if good fortune allows,

but I must find this Barbur
in secret somehow.

We're part of a coven and all in the fold,

allied with alchemy
in the search for new gold.

I wish life was different and that I was free;

if only I had
sweet Bela with me.

But it's back to my purpose or my Clarice shall scold,

for I'm still running errands,
forced to do as I'm told.

Narrator (Hiding in the Eaves)

Poor Fabian, the errand boy
    his thoughts are manyfold,

though surely he must ponder hard
    on his father's quest for gold.

Poor Richard, our alchemist,
    who worries day and night,

seeking fortune more than fame
    must get that mixture right.

They have arranged a meeting
    in a back-room at The Star,

but Richard's funds are running low
    "Success," he says, "not far."

Fabian has other hopes,
    for Bela might appear -

I have my place within the eaves
    so we may overhear.

Gold (Part 3)

Fabian to Richard Barbur:

At last, we meet in secret here -
my father sends a message clear:

your benefactors all await
the golden linings of their fate.

In silver coin they have been fair
and all request their final share.

So one report I must take back:
'success is ours' - for funds we lack!

This room is ours until we go
but we shall keep our voices low.

Be not afraid of spies within -
I know the owners and their kin.

Speak freely, tell me Richard, true,
do dreams of riches rest with you?

Shall fame and fortune fall my way
and ladies seek me night and day,

or shall these tiny threads of gold
snap like winter's shards so cold?

Gold (Part 4)

Richard Barbur to Fabian:
'Tis not as easy as some think!
Both day *and* night in smoke and stink,

I slave to brighten up your lives -
all mistresses and wealth and wives,

bathed in jewels from head to toe
purchased by my precious gold.

Patience, please, some patience, all,
and soon you'll hear my clarion call.

The house is watched - I've seen them all
- they loiter by the market stalls,

they follow me around the town
disguised with hood or cap or gown;

some bear a staff, and others sacks -
I know that they will soon attack!

I have the means, ingredients, all,
to concentrate and gently call

upon my wits to mix them well,
and when 'tis done, my friends I'll tell.

Now I must leave here after you,
disguised once more in blackest hues.

Scorpio

I see that Dizzy's watching me -
he begs by Greyfriar's gate,
I must move on and out of sight
or else be tempting fate.

Warwick's merchants come this way
and we have spies who tell
of secret meetings at strange hours,
which we think bodes us well.

There is a web which we all know
that we shall soon expose,
and take the gold and so much more
from underneath its nose!

We'll slip away to distant parts -
avoid the hue and cry,
and live our lives in finery
and comfort, by and by.

We wonder who the spider is
that weaves this web so tight,
for we have watchmen everywhere
at gates both day and night.

Mayhap it matters not at all
when gold and gossamer's gone,
for we shall all the richer be
as Kings, no longer pawns!

Jabet's Ash (Part 1)

Bela to Fabian:

I'll see you nearby Jabet's Ash -
go out past Gosford Gate,

but take good care to hide your face,
and best that you aren't late.

You spluttered you have tales to tell
and things you have to say,

but I no longer dream of you,
nor think of you each day.

If Maud or Addy do suspect,
they will some trouble make,

but mostly wish to 'coddle me
just for this baby's sake.

I see your wife looks round and well
upon her horse so fine -

methinks one day we both shall meet
near St Osburga's shrine.

So, meet me up by Jabet's Ash
not far from Gosford Gate,

where I shall listen carefully
and then decide your fate.

When Fortune Smiles

Addy (quietly to himself):
When Fortune smiles we must look up
and thank the Lord above -
a moment's peace to sit and think
on all of those I love.

My Maud she was the brightest light
- my torch on darkest days;
my heart did break with silent tears
the day we parted ways.

The war was long, the battles fierce,
but I did hope to see
the Maud that I had left behind
in fair old Coventry.

When I returned, The Star was hers
her ales could not be bettered;
she always was a clever one,
and even learned her letters.

Now years have passed, this secret's mine
that she has shared with me,
and though I've wished it many times,
I must confess my glee;

for Bela is a child of joy,
her smile is sunshine pure,
and I have loved her all these days -
it always shall endure.

I hope it's soon we're side by side
and I shall draw her near,
and whisper 'daughter' in her ear
and say I love her dear.

Jabet's Ash (Part 2)

Fabian to Bela:

Oh, Bela my beloved,
we must be more discreet,
for whispers lead to other things
when you and I do meet.

Oh, Bela my beloved,
I shall explain to you
'twas duty forced my hand on hers,
though all my love's for you.

Oh, Bela my beloved,
it grieves me very hard,
ah, the memory of our final kiss
in that moonlit stable-yard.

Oh, Bela my beloved,
this truth I speak laid bare,
and you must know 'tis family ties
which now have me ensnared.

Oh, Bela my beloved,
I must now take your leave.
Queen of my heart you shall remain,
and that you must believe!

Oh, Bela my beloved,
I hope our paths may cross,
should you go near my manor lands
near Stretton-under-Fosse.

Jabet's Ash (Part 3)

Bela to Fabian:

Your beloved no longer, so much stronger am I,
for my heart is now free and soars in the sky.

I danced for your pennies, instead of rich jewels;
not thinking that you might have me for a fool.

Your beloved no longer, so much stronger am I,
for my heart is now free and soars in the sky.

My love was as gold, so precious and rare,
which I gave to you freely, believing you'd care.

Your beloved no longer, so much stronger am I,
for my heart is now free and soars in the sky.

I took all your promises and set them on fire
when I did discover that you were a liar!

Your beloved no longer, so much stronger am I,
for my heart is now free and soars in the sky.

So, this is the last time that we shall both meet,
but your wife does look pretty and her I shall greet!

Your beloved no longer, so much stronger am I,
for my heart is now free and soars in the sky.

Sagittarius

I wish I had my arrows,
I would use them here and now -
I am so tired of waiting 'round,
though I'd never break my vow.

I miss the thrill of hunt and chase
with all my skills on show,
but day and night I must stay put
to see who comes and goes.

How I wish I had my arrows,
I would use them here and now -
I am so tired of waiting 'round
though I'd never break my vow.

The Captain's views are different -
he tells us to be calm,
and bide our time, then seize the gold,
avoid the need to harm.

But I wish I had my arrows,
I would use them here and now -
I am so tired of waiting 'round,
though I'd never break my vow.

I could charge in with bow a-fire,
let my comrades see me work,
but our Captain plays a patient game,
so in shadows I must lurk.

Oh, how I wish I had my arrows -
I would use them here and now -
I get so tired of waiting 'round,
though I'd never break my vow.

Narrator (Counting Blessings)

The son and heir with broken heart
    I see has lost his charms.

No longer Bela by his side,
    but Clarice on his arm.

Lamenting o'er his family life
    he's wealthier than most,

he's noticed not conspirators
    who shadow him like ghosts.

He should take care, for wealth may fail
    when Fortune's wheel has spun;

counting blessings, wife with child -
    a family life begun,

with land and riches, more to come
    if alchemy be good,

just be content with thanks to God
    and watch out for those hoods!

See how they follow closer now,
    but do not make to steal;

intent upon their Captain's words
    they must hold to their deal.

Who knows how this will all turn out?
    Dear reader, ask me not,

for I can only play the part I'm given
    while some devise and plot.

Among The Stars

Fabian laments:
Oh, where among the constellations
is there sparkle matching hers?
If duties could be damned
we'd be a-bed adorned with furs.

I feel that I have dropped an owche
with jewels gleaming bright -
upon the path of fate 'twas lost,
forever gone from sight.

Now where among the constellations
is there sparkle matching hers?
If duties could be damned
we'd be a-bed adorned with furs.

But a family's honour must hold higher
than the rules of common folk,
and I must live the life I'm given -
with best cloths and finest cloaks.

But where among the constellations
is there sparkle matching hers?
If duties could be damned
we'd be a-bed adorned with furs.

A wife, and soon a child, will mean
a family new, oh yes,
all done to grant my father's wishes
though he would never guess

that I was searching constellations
for a sparkle matching hers,
for if duties could be damned
we'd be a-bed adorned with furs.

Farewell

Jocelin sings:

No tears, my dove, my beauty Queen;
farewell, my love, farewell.

For we have dreamed our lovers' dream;
farewell, my love, farewell.

'Tis time for night's delights to end;
farewell, my love, farewell.

'Tis time for hearts at last to mend;
farewell, my love, farewell.

I will foreswear your company;
farewell, my love, farewell.

For you are bound and not yet free;
farewell my love, farewell.

One day, sweetheart, when love rings true;
farewell, my love, farewell.

I shall not sing these words to you:
farewell, my love, farewell.

Gold (Part 5)

Richard Barbur:

Dear reader, keep a watch for me
as I walk home through Coventry.
I've seen men's shadows, nine thus far,
the last one just outside The Star!

I trust you, friends, beyond all doubt,
so if you see them, please do shout.
These legs of mine no longer run -
but chasing me, for them, is fun.

They seek all I know, for I'm their man;
to capture me is in their plan!

Dear reader, if you're still watching I'll catch my breath ...

... for in Cambridge I once lived, quite happy in that town,
and mingled all the while among the caps and gowns,

carried out experiments - I would have stayed on my own
but then would need to borrow more in many, many loans.

So here I am a frightened man and in a fearful state,
pursued by all my foes and aides who simply cannot wait!

But now perchance I see my home, I'll quicken up at last,
so I shall I make my entrance sly, and hopefully quite fast;

it's through a secret door I'll pass, and only I shall know,
so please don't look, for heaven's sake, 'tis time for me to go!

Narrator (The Air is Clear)

The air is clear in parts up here
    the smoke and smell aside;
our alchemist is home at last
    but has no place to hide.

Perched high upon my viewing branch
    I saw the note slide through
that door's small crack above the step -
    the alchemist sees too.

Who knows what twists and turns await
    our fellowship of gold?
Will Richard's alchemy break down
    the barriers that scold?

Mayhap young Fabian will see his life
    is rich enough already
But somewhere in the midst of all
    our plotters seem unsteady.

Jocelin and Bela now
    have found each other's hand,
Maud and Addy watching close
    will hope all goes as planned.

'Tis time to let the players play
    and let the story be;
'tis time to find another perch
    and see what I can see.

Capricorn

'Don't linger near the lepers', that's what they said to me -
I'm keeping well away from them
while I'm in Coventry!

Our Captain sent a message and I answered when I could,
now I'm disguised and hobble thus
with staff and cloak and hood.

'Don't linger near the lepers', that's what they said to me -
I'm keeping well away from them
while I'm in Coventry!

My hiding place is near Spon Cross and Hill Street; I can see
if anyone who's on our list
is come to Coventry!

'Don't linger near the lepers', that's what they said to me -
I'm keeping well away from them
while I'm in Coventry!

I hear the brook a-babbling when Radford's mill is still,
and listen to the birdsong sweet
when I have had my fill.

'Don't linger near the lepers', that's what they said to me -
I'm keeping well away from them
while I'm in Coventry!

The Sherbourne flows like mercy, its water pure and clear,
I watch the fish go swimming by
and wish I'd brough my spear!

'Don't linger near the lepers', that's what they said to me -
I'm keeping well away from them
while I'm in Coventry!

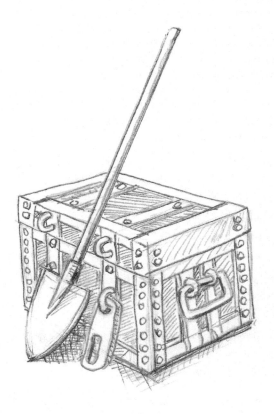

Bury All Deep

Richard Barbur:

I've picked up this note and it's threatening me -
to give up my secrets and set them all free!

Is somebody watching? Is anyone there?
I now know that someone is taking great care

to find all my footsteps and see where I go,
observing each purchase to seek what I know.

But I'll dig a big hole and bury all deep,
and buy me some dogs to guard while I sleep.

Somethings afoot - there's a hint in the air
I shall draw out my horoscope to see what's in there.

Those beggars can plot while sat on their stools,
but should they assail me I'll have them for fools!

For I'll dig a big hole and bury all deep,
and buy me some dogs to guard while I sleep.

My patrons shall know of this mischievous plan -
with friends in high places and guardians on hand;

methinks they will offer a strong-box with locks,
and labour with shovels to look after their stock,

and we'll dig a big hole to bury all deep,
then buy me some dogs to guard while I sleep.

Aquarius

Here at Cheylesmore Manor,
it suits me very well;
a stationed house and comely home
for this tousle-haired Tyrell.

A lowly maiden's all
that others 'round can see,

I fetch or else I carry,
but at least I am quite free

to come and go just as I please,
to watch and also listen,

to pick up pearls or even scraps,
and notice eyes that glisten;

I note down hurried footsteps,
a drape that oft-times twitches,

when sneaky reeve and buxom cook
are scratching sinful itches!

Yes, here at Cheylesmore Manor,
it suits me very well;
a stationed house and comely home
for this tousle-haired Tyrell.

Limbrick Wood (Part 1)

Message to John Jabet from a co-conspirator:
I'll meet you out by Limbrick Wood,
but in disguise with cowl or hood.

Be ready, though, for trails that follow -
the pledge of some mayhap be hollow;

I know my own and trust their word,
but in the shadows doubts are heard

from latecomers to our company,
those friends of friends in Coventry.

We'll speak much more of these concerns -
our plot may have more twists and turns,

so keep our footing sure and steady,
should one betray, we must be ready!

This night at nine by Limbrick Wood,
but in disguise with cowl and hood!

Pisces

I'm poaching by Swanswell pool, as it
ripples under a waning moonrise.
It has been a long day and I'm hungry.

The Captain gave me this star sign,
so I hope for some good fortune and
a fish to fill my belly. I still have some
ale to wash it down with.

I did bring news to share, but curfew came
before I could be within the city walls.

Ah, here's the bait. I learned as a boy to
stick to the shadows, stay out of sight,
be still and patient - just what I've been doing
for days before finally hearing a name spoken
too loudly. Carried on the breeze, 'twas
like a lovely melody to mine ears!

I can tell no-one until I tell our Captain,
for we were well-drilled and I have no desire
to lose half my share for not following rules.

And now I feel the tug of the line I see
that night's fortune follows the day's!

Limbrick Wood (Part 2)

Message from John Jabet to a co-conspirator:

I've had my doubts on one or two -
by Limbrick Wood we'll sort them through.

I'll be disguised with cowl and cloak
and meet you by the broadest oak.

My skills are such that none shall trail -
if some do try, they all shall fail!

Our zodiac, twelve folk thought true,
some picked by me, some picked by you.

But others we have not known long
weak with sword, more keen on songs!

Curse them for their feeble minds
oh, we shall punish come the time!

The strong we'll keep close by our side,
for we shall need them by and by.

We are so close - not quite complete ...
but this may bring us near defeat!

This night at nine by Limbrick Wood -
unmask our fears with cowl and hood!

Riddle I Can Solve

Addy confronts John Jabet:

John Jabet, please, lay down your arms -
no-one shall come to any harm.

No use in spoiling for a fight,
my men will take you back this night.

The gaol is ready, all prepared,
the note we sent has you ensnared.

Surprised to see your fall from grace?
I see that look upon your face.

Your plot has been uncovered, yes,
and time will come when all's confessed.

Oh we have others in this game -
with zodiac and proper name!

You have questions, by and by,
they are dancing in your eyes.

Why not wait until the deed is done -
catch you while you're having fun?

Now there's a riddle I can solve
easier than a priest absolves.

Barbur's protected by our King,
so we must break your plotter's ring.

The King, we're told, will soon be here:
alchemy's gold will bring him cheer!

Narrator (Story's Ending)

And now we see this story's ending;
    some things are broken, hearts are mending.

The *Wheel of Fortune* turns once more
    at the slam of the gaol's iron door.

Duty, home and hearth do call -
    Fabian with wife ride beyond our walls.

The King and Queen shall soon be met -
    our own Leet Court have plans to set.

The Prior will never be out-done
    and plots away to have his fun -

Odo's his man, so all watch out,
    when raising funds he lowers his snout.

Before I take my leave, retire,
    and fly up to my favourite spire,

I leave you, friends, with song at *The Star*
    and wish you good health wherever you are!

Felicity of My Heart

Jocelin sings:

In summer's blaze or darker days,
I'm drawn to you in many ways,
felicity of my heart.

On starlit nights with frost that bites,
your warmth brings light,
felicity of my heart.

So pale be all those candle-flames
while I am in your gentle arms,
felicity of my heart.

Let others stare at beauty rare,
for thou art so very, very fair,
felicity of my heart.

And all the while I am beguiled
by endless sunshine-bringing smiles,
felicity of my heart.

Let not a single moment pass me by
without you close, here at my side,
felicity of my heart.

And may Almighty God let it forever be,
my love with you and yours with me,
felicity of my heart.

Author's Notes

Historical Characters

The Golden Thread is set in and around the year 1450, but I have taken some liberties with time-frames in using characters based on real people. The *Leet Book* was my source for non-fictional names. I had some luck regarding Richard Barbur, the alchemist - his name and occupation popped up when I was reading looking for names and events that might spark a storyline.

Richard lived in St Nicholas' Street in Coventry (in the 1470s), and appears to have had royal protection. The King (being in constant need of gold) clearly wanted to look after those who aspired to (or claimed that they could!) create gold from the base elements.

John Jabet is recorded as living in Bishop Street in 1449 and I used the name so that I could have Jabet's Ash as a setting. There is some dispute as to where the name came from, but today's Jabet's Ash was cultivated from a *previous* Jabet's Ash tree that grew on what is now the Binley Road in Coventry. The tree was apparently used as a meeting point for dignitaries coming from Leicester - they would then be guided or led into the City via the appropriate gate (Gosford Gate would have been the closest one).

Spicer Stoke was primarily a small row of grocers' shops and dwellings between Holy Trinity Church and Butcher Row (*spicer* is a medieval term for *grocer*). There is a photograph of Spicer Stoke Gate in Coventry's Herbert Museum Reference Library, most likely taken when redeveloping the city after World War II.

The Medieval name for Limbrick Wood was 'Lingbok' - 'Linge' being Celtic - *'Llyn'* meaning *'liquid* or *water'* and *'cain'* meaning *'clear'*, hence *'Limbrick'* - 'The brook with clear water' (for more details, please see http://tilehillkid.uk/).

References

Below are some useful references used when writing *The Golden Thread*, with individual vignettes of wonder. Some may only be visible via a reference library, so I have included online references which offer an alternative.

1. *The Coventry Leet Book (or Mayor's Register)*, transcribed and edited by Mary Dormer Harris. Published 1907 by Kegan Paul, Trench, Trübner & Co. Ltd.
2. An Internet Version of *The Coventry Leet Book* can be found by some targeted searching for it at this website: https://archive.org/
3. *The Story of Coventry* by Mary Dormer Harris, published 1911 by J M Dent & Sons Ltd.
4. Internet Version of *The Story of Coventry* can be found by searching for *Mary Dormer Harris* at this website: https://www.gutenberg.org/
5. *Dr Troughton's Sketches of Old Coventry* by Dr Nathaniel Troughton. Publication date unknown, published by B T Batsford (London).
6. *Coventry's Heritage* by Levi Fox, published (second edition) 1957 by The Coventry Evening Telegraph.
7. *Coventry - Echoes of the Past* by Frank Roden, published 1984 by Coral Productions.
8. *The Little History Of Coventry* by Peter Walters, published 2019 by The History Press.
9. *The Canterbury Tales* by Geoffrey Chaucer, published 1901 by Gay & Bird.
10. *The Wharncliffe Companion To Coventry* by David McGrory, published 2008 by Wharncliffe Books.
11. *The Victoria History Of The County Of Warwick* (Volume VIII) by University Of London Institute Of Historical Research, published 1969 by Oxford University Press.

12. Historic Coventry website:
    https://www.historiccoventry.co.uk/main/main.php
13. Medieval Coventry website:
    http://medievalcoventry.co.uk/
14. Local History website:
    http://tilehillkid.uk/

About the Author

Paul lives and works in Coventry and has published several poetry collections. In Royal Leamington Spa Gallery, he was poet-in-residence at the *Concealment & Deception* exhibition and *Guest Poet* in celebrating International Poetry Day. Paul has also been privileged to share his poetry at St John The Baptist Church in Fleet Street, Coventry, within their *Festival of Peace & Reconciliation* for November's Remembrance Days. Paul was guest poet at Coventry's Central Library to launch his World War I book *Journey To The Front*.

Try finding Paul on Facebook under *Paul-AM-Palmer-Poetry*, or on X (Twitter), or via his blog – links are below.

http://twitter.com/paulpalmerpoet

http://paulampalmer.wordpress.com

About the Illustrator

Paul and Steve met when they were students at Coventry Lanchester Polytechnic (now Coventry University). Steve gained a degree in Fine Art, before returning to his native Yorkshire to begin a career as a nurse. Now retired, he enjoys having more time to dabble in art again.

Other Books by Paul A M Palmer:

Boys On The Battlefield - Published by CreateSpace (2015)
ISBN-13: 978- 1511408837

Who Will Carry Me? - Published by CreateSpace (2015)
ISBN-13: 978-1508672920

Shelling Peas - Published by CreateSpace (2015)
ISBN-13: 978-1511499309

Sea Of Hands - Published by CreateSpace (2016)
ISBN-13: 978-1542436526

Watching The Sand - Published by CreateSpace (2017)
ISBN-13: 978-1542436526

Journey To The Front - Published by CreateSpace (2018)
ISBN-13:978-1530278909

Perspective - Published by CreateSpace (2018)
ISBN-13: 978-1979700610

Locked In - Published by Kindle Desktop Publishing (2019)
ISBN-13: 978-1722161224

A Coventry Tale ... woven in poetry - Published by Kindle Desktop Publishing (2020)
ISBN-13: 979-8668499526.

Getting The Story Out - Published by Kindle Desktop Publishing (2021)
ISBN-13: 979-8574310588.

Printed in Great Britain
by Amazon